The Seaside

by Annabelle Lynch

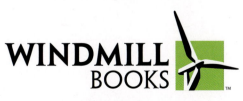

New York

Published in 2016 by **Windmill Books**,
an Imprint of Rosen Publishing
29 East 21st Street, New York, NY 10010

Copyright © 2016 The Watts Publishing Group/Windmill

All rights reserved. No part of this book may be reproduced in any form without permission in writing from the publisher, except by a reviewer.

Series editor: Julia Bird
Series consultant: Catherine Glavina
Series designer: Peter Scoulding

Photo Credits: Peter Chadwick/Gallo Images/Alamy: 13, 22cl. Melissa Anne Colors/Shutterstock: 8-9, 22bl. James Forte/National Geographic/Alamy: 1, 12, 22tl. Gledriiis/Shutterstock: 14-15. GoBob/Shutterstock: 6-7, 22cr. ksl/Shutterstock: 18-19, 22cla. MartiniDry/Shutterstock: 4-5, 22br. Rolf Schlegel/Alamy: front cover. Vilaincrevette/Shutterstock: 16-17, 22tr. Yobro10/Dreamstime: 20-21. Feng Yu/Shutterstock: 10-11.

Cataloging-in-Publication Data

Lynch, Annabelle.
The seaside / by Annabelle Lynch.
p. cm. — (Nature explorers)
Includes index.
ISBN 978-1-5081-9073-8 (pbk.)
ISBN 978-1-5081-9074-5 (6-pack)
ISBN 978-1-5081-9075-2 (library binding)
1. Seashore — Juvenile literature. 2. Seashore ecology — Juvenile literature. 3. Seashore biology — Juvenile literature. I. Lynch, Annabelle. II. Title.
QH95.7 L96 2016
578.769'9—d23

Manufactured in the United States of America
CPSIA Compliance Information: Batch #BW16PK: For Further Information
contact Rosen Publishing, New York, New York at 1-800-237-9932

Contents

The seaside!	4
Sand or pebbles?	6
Shells	8
Tides	10
Rock pools	13
Seabirds	14
Fish in the sea	16
Boats	18
Seaside fun	20
Word bank	22
Quiz	23
Notes, answers, and index	24

The seaside!

The seaside is where land and sea meet.

Sand or pebbles?

The seaside can have sand, rocks, or pebbles.

Shells

You can find shells at the seaside.

Tides

At the seaside, the tide comes in and goes out every day.

Rock pools

When the tide is out, you can see rock pools. Animals live in them.

Crab

Seabirds

Birds live at the seaside. They catch crabs and fish to eat.

Fish in the sea

All sorts of fish live in the sea. Many live near coral reefs.

Boats

Boats carry people on the sea. Ferries carry lots of people.

Seaside fun

Have fun at the seaside.
Splash in the sea or
build a sand castle!

Word bank

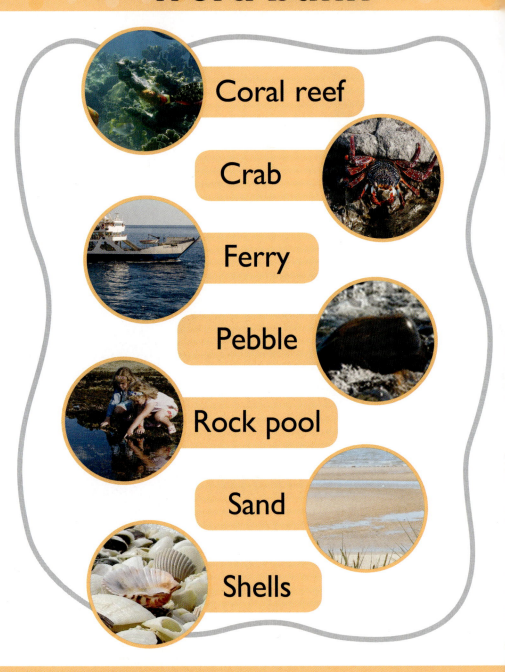

Quiz

1. At the seaside, you can find

a) shells
b) sausages
c) socks

2. The tide goes

a) up and down
b) in and out
c) around and around

3. Ferries carry lots of

a) fish
b) frogs
c) people

Turn over for answers!

Notes for parents and teachers

Nature Explorers are structured to provide support for newly independent readers. The books may also be used by adults for sharing with young children.

Starting to read alone can be daunting. **Nature Explorers** help by providing visual support and repeating words and phrases. These books will both develop confidence and encourage reading and rereading for pleasure.

If you are reading this book with a child, here are a few suggestions:
1. Make reading fun! Choose a time to read when you and the child are relaxed and have time to share the book.
2. Talk about the content of the book before you start reading. Look at the front cover. What expectations are raised about the content? Why might the child enjoy it? What connections can the child make with their own experience of the world?
3. If a word is phonically decodable, encourage the child to use a "phonics first" approach to tackling new words by sounding the words out.
4. Invite the child to talk about the content after reading, returning to favorite pages and pictures. Extend vocabulary by examining the Word Bank and by discussing new concepts.
5. Give praise! Remember that small mistakes need not always be corrected.

Answers

Here are the answers:

1. a   2. b   3. c

Index

birds 14
boats 19
coral reefs 17
ferries 19
fish 14, 17

rock pools 13
sand 6
shells 9
tide 11, 13

Quiz

1. At the seaside, you can find

a) shells
b) sausages
c) socks

2. The tide goes

a) up and down
b) in and out
c) around and around

3. Ferries carry lots of

a) fish
b) frogs
c) people

Turn over for answers!

Notes for parents and teachers

Nature Explorers are structured to provide support for newly independent readers. The books may also be used by adults for sharing with young children.

Starting to read alone can be daunting. **Nature Explorers** help by providing visual support and repeating words and phrases. These books will both develop confidence and encourage reading and rereading for pleasure.

If you are reading this book with a child, here are a few suggestions:
1. Make reading fun! Choose a time to read when you and the child are relaxed and have time to share the book.
2. Talk about the content of the book before you start reading. Look at the front cover. What expectations are raised about the content? Why might the child enjoy it? What connections can the child make with their own experience of the world?
3. If a word is phonically decodable, encourage the child to use a "phonics first" approach to tackling new words by sounding the words out.
4. Invite the child to talk about the content after reading, returning to favorite pages and pictures. Extend vocabulary by examining the Word Bank and by discussing new concepts.
5. Give praise! Remember that small mistakes need not always be corrected.

Answers

Here are the answers:

1. a   2. b   3. c

Index

birds 14
boats 19
coral reefs 17
ferries 19
fish 14, 17

rock pools 13
sand 6
shells 9
tide 11, 13